Copyright © 2012 by Rubina Reierson
First Edition – July 2012

ISBN
978-1-77097-354-1 (Paperback)

All rights reserved.

No part of this publication may be reproduced in any form, or by any means, electronic or mechanical, including photocopying, recording, or any information browsing, storage, or retrieval system, without permission in writing from the publisher.

Published by:

FriesenPress
Suite 300 – 852 Fort Street
Victoria, BC, Canada V8W 1H8

www.friesenpress.com

Distributed to the trade by The Ingram Book Company

The nine members that formed the first Local Spiritual Assembly in Fraser Lake, BC in the spring of 1984

My Spiritual Journey that led me to find the Bahá'í Faith was a yearning that started when I was about twelve years old. It was at that time that I had a desire to talk about the nature of God, and try and make sense of why a loving God would allow such pain and suffering on this earth. I was raised in a family of eleven children, I was the seventh and last child born at home on a homestead in northern Saskatchewan, Canada.

My parents moved around to different Canadian locations before they settled in Prince George, British Columbia in 1952. We later moved to the nearby town of Vanderhoof, where I eventually met my future husband, we got married, and during the next twelve years we were blessed with five children, whom were all born in Vanderhoof.

As the years passed I would read all the spiritual books that I could find. Then in 1972, I experienced a spiritual encounter with my higher self, but at the time I couldn't find words to explain what had taken place during my sleeping hours. More years passed and as I read more books on the metaphysical line of thought I became more enlightened as to what had taken place those many years before. Now, in my later years, I found the book "A Course in Miracles" which explained my experience in words that I couldn't explain back then. This is what took place as close as I can explain: After prayer I fell asleep, but it felt as though I was awake and conscious. It felt as though I was being drawn without walking into a very bright light that was as bright as the sun, yet didn't hurt my eyesight. I remember great fear, as I was propelled into the light. Then when I came in contact with the light, a feeling of complete love and peace overwhelmed me, which words cannot describe.

In the book A Course in Miracles it states:

"Everyone has experienced what he would call a sense of being transported beyond himself. This feeling of liberation far exceeds the dream of freedom sometimes hoped for in special relationships. It is a sense of actual escape from liberations. If you will consider what this "*transportation*" really entails, you will realize that it is a sudden unawareness of the body, and a joining of yourself and something else in which your mind enlarges to encompass it. It becomes a part of you, as you unite with it. And both become whole, as neither is perceived as separate. What really happens is that you have given up the illusion of a limited awareness, and lost your fear of union. The love that instantly replaces it extends to what has freed you, and unites with it. And while this lasts you are not uncertain of your Identity, and would not limit it. You have escaped from fear to peace, asking no questions of reality, but merely accepting it. You have accepted this instead of the body, and have let yourself be one with something beyond it, simply by not letting your mind be limited by it... Yet in every case, you join it without reservation because you love it, and would be with it, and so you rush to meet it, letting your limits melt away, suspending all the "laws" your body obeys and gently setting them aside." (Schucman, 2007, p.387).

This was truly an out of the body experience for me at that time, but my journey for truth was only beginning as I read more books and studied about different world religions.

A few years later I became best friends with my neighbor. She introduced me to a broader viewpoint of thinking. I will always remember when she said "When the student is ready the teacher will appear".

Now a whole new world had opened up for me. I ordered books from a book store in Vancouver, books of Science and Theology by H.P. Blavatsky, and books by Vera Stanley Alder that gave clear understanding of science and the body. I studied the Unity Faith and found it very satisfying.

In 1975 we moved to the north shore of Fraser Lake. A friend of our daughter invited us to a "Fireside". I didn't know what that was at the time, so I asked. She explained that it was a gathering of like-minded people that got together to socialize, and read and discuss writings about the Bahá'í Faith. This was a good opportunity for me to find out what this Faith had to offer. Well, to my surprise this was the path that I was searching for at that time on my spiritual journey. The Bahá'í Faith teaches the Principles that mankind needs: The oneness of God, mankind and religion. The equality of men and women. Harmony of science and religion. Elimination of extremes of wealth and poverty. Universal peace. Universal education and independent search of truth.

This Faith came to be manifested through The Báb in 1844. He was a young merchant from Shíráz, Persia (now Iran), who began to teach these principles which were a hindrance to the priesthood and church-state of Persia.

He taught that a new spiritual era was at hand. Soon he had many devoted followers which led to his imprisonment and systematic massacres of His followers. The Báb promised that God would send a new manifestation in nineteen years that would begin to teach the basic laws and principles for a new age.

A few years later in 1984 I signed my declaration card and accepted the Baha'i teachings as my faith. I truly believed that Bahá'u'lláh, (meaning "Glory of God"), The One whom the Báb promised would come, was who He declared to be: A Messenger sent by God.

As we now had nine believers in that community, I was a part of the first Local Spiritual Assembly in Fraser Lake. BC. It takes nine believers in the faith to form a Local Spiritual Assembly and any number lower than nine automatically becomes a group, which did eventually occur as a few members later moved away.

About five years later I acquired a virus, later to be diagnosed as "Sarcoidosis". Some of the symptoms were on the level of lupus; which is an autoimmune disease which can lead to organ damage; it was truly a disabling experience. As a result, I spent a lot of time in my recliner with my feet up, studying the writings of Bahá'u'lláh. As the weeks went by, I started writing verses about the history of the Bahá'í Faith. Soon I found I had a ballad about the life and teachings of the Faith.

This all took place while we lived in Fraser Lake, and when my husband retired we moved to the Okanagan, to where our children had previously moved. We attended Bahá'í summer schools with our family, and many functions with friends of the Faith.

This year in Nov. 2011, I decided to publish my Ballad that I had written before our move to the Okanagan. This Ballad and these words, I leave as a legacy to my husband, our children, grandchildren, and great grandchildren; and all humanity.

With all my Love,
Rubina Reierson.

REFERENCES

Schucman, Helen and Thetford, William. (2007). A Course in Miracles (Third Edition). California: Foundation for Inner Peace.

These beautiful 9-pointed stars were created by
Gary Stewart *at www.freewebs.com/bahaistars/*

Ballad of the Bahá'í Faith

In the land of Persia, far over the sea,

From the city of Shiráz came He,

Mohammed had foretold the Madhi would come,

The Báb had declared it was He.

On the twenty-third of May,
in eighteen forty-four,

Very near that special morn,

The Báb declared His mission,

And 'Abdu'l-Bahá was born.

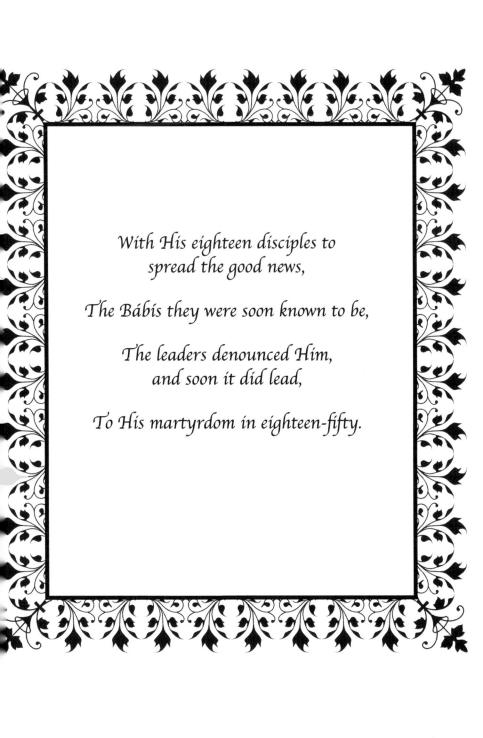

With His eighteen disciples to
spread the good news,

The Bábís they were soon known to be,

The leaders denounced Him,
and soon it did lead,

To His martyrdom in eighteen-fifty.

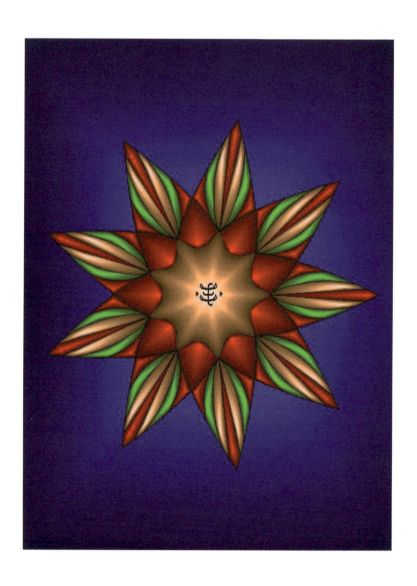

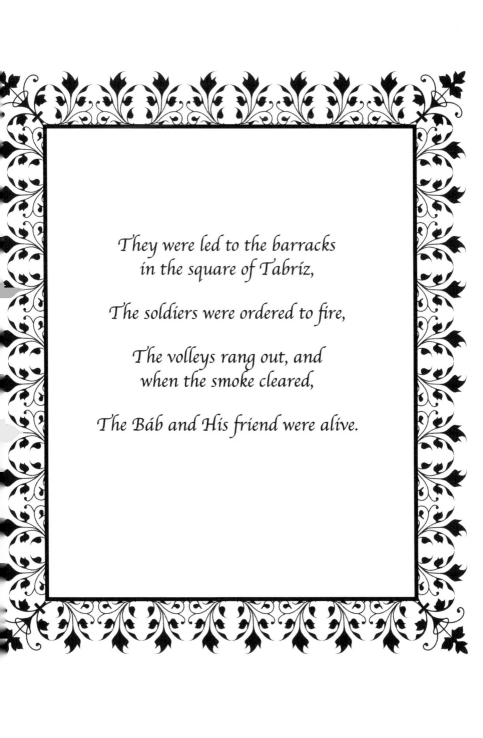

They were led to the barracks
in the square of Tabríz,

The soldiers were ordered to fire,

The volleys rang out, and
when the smoke cleared,

The Báb and His friend were alive.

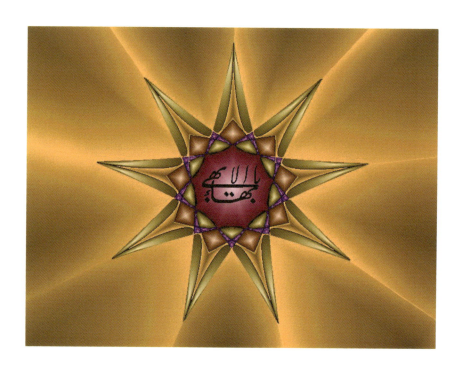

On this hot day, on the Ninth of July,

They were ordered to finish the job,

The ones that had aimed, a miracle claimed,

So others ended the life of the Báb.

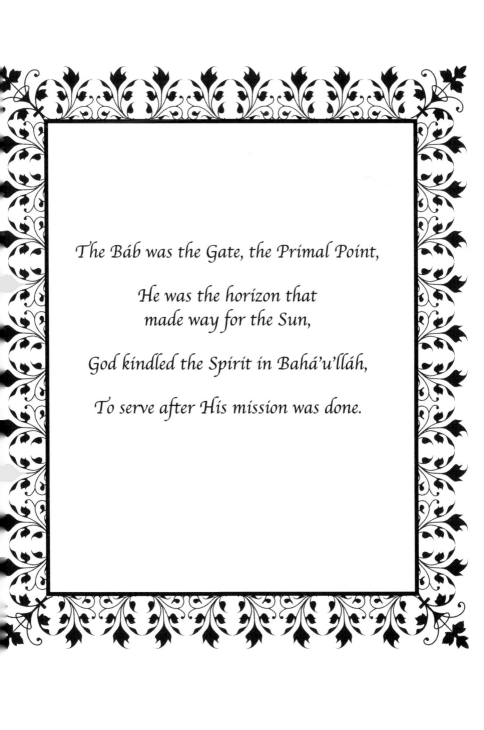

The Báb was the Gate, the Primal Point,

He was the horizon that
made way for the Sun,

God kindled the Spirit in Bahá'u'lláh,

To serve after His mission was done.

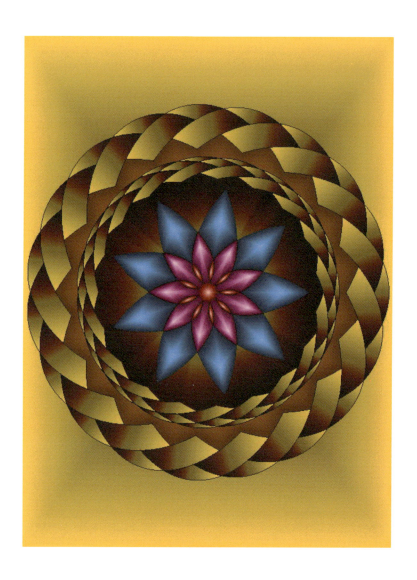

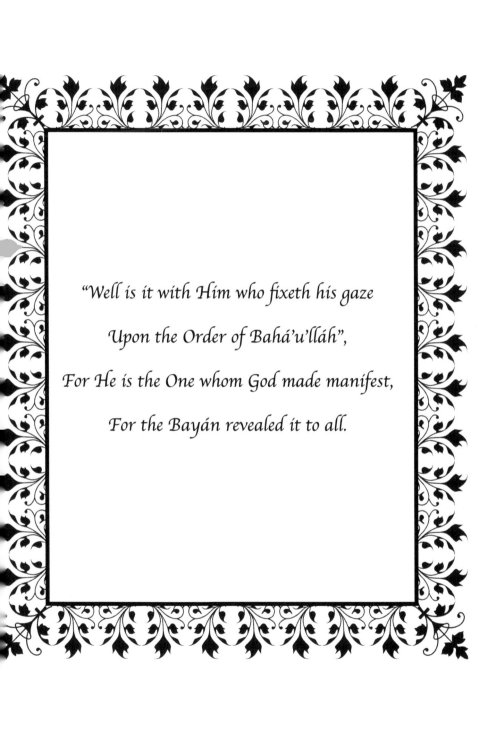

"Well is it with Him who fixeth his gaze

Upon the Order of Bahá'u'lláh",

For He is the One whom God made manifest,

For the Bayán revealed it to all.

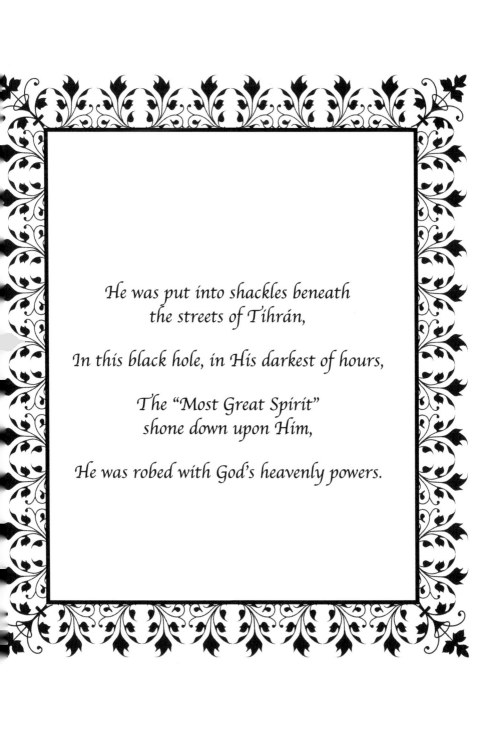

He was put into shackles beneath
the streets of Tihrán,

In this black hole, in His darkest of hours,

The "Most Great Spirit"
shone down upon Him,

He was robed with God's heavenly powers.

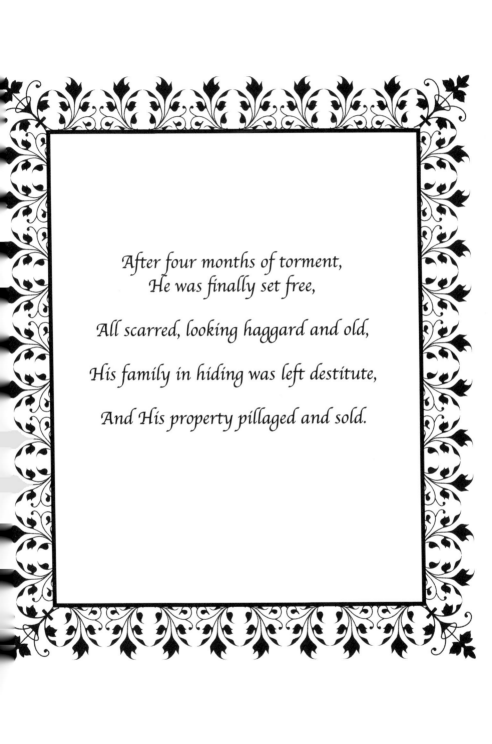

After four months of torment,
He was finally set free,

All scarred, looking haggard and old,

His family in hiding was left destitute,

And His property pillaged and sold.

He was banned from his home-
land, exiled to Baghdád,

His soul then began to unfold,

With newly found wisdom,
and spiritual power,

His secret not yet to be told.

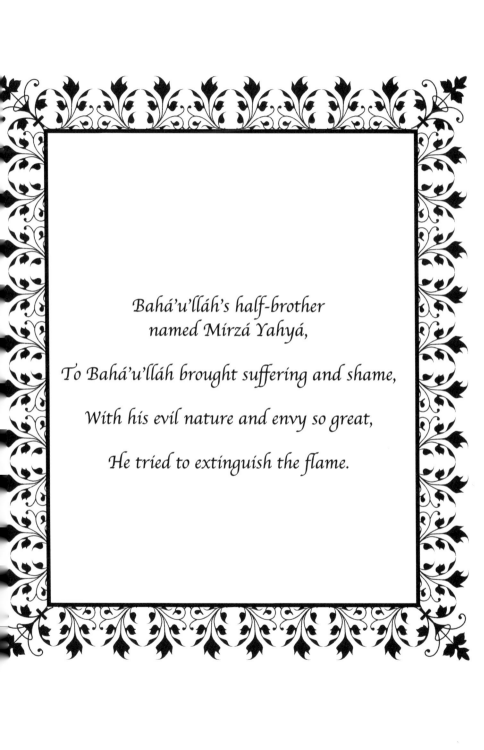

Bahá'u'lláh's half-brother
named Mirzá Yahyá,

To Bahá'u'lláh brought suffering and shame,

With his evil nature and envy so great,

He tried to extinguish the flame.

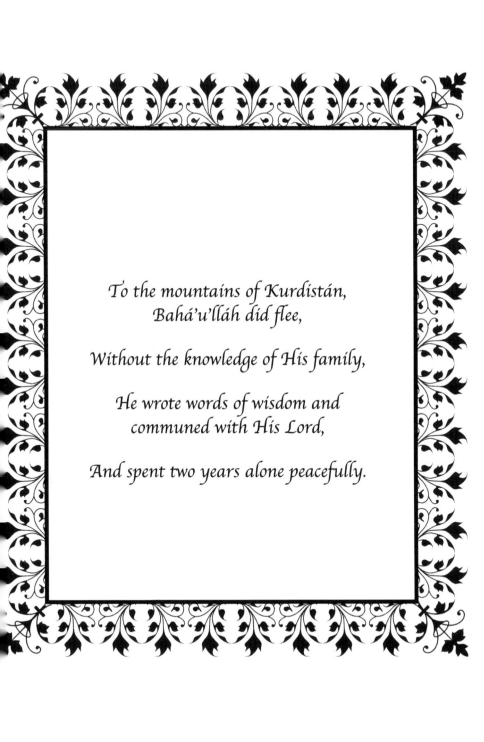

To the mountains of Kurdistán,
Bahá'u'lláh did flee,

Without the knowledge of His family,

He wrote words of wisdom and
communed with His Lord,

And spent two years alone peacefully.

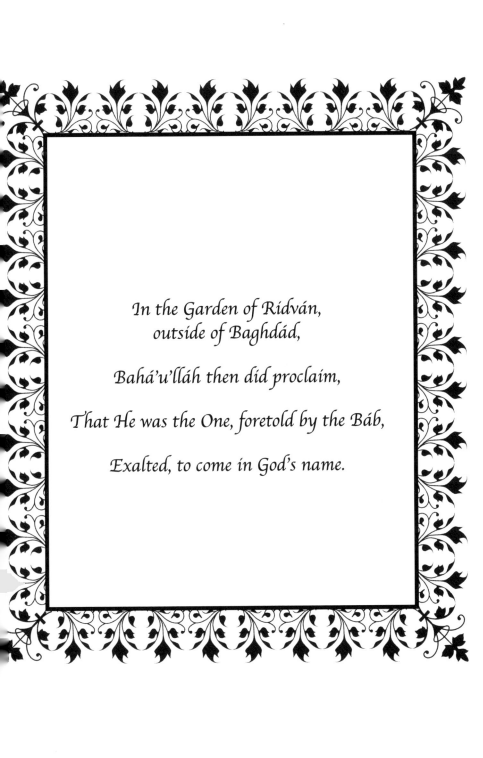

In the Garden of Rídván,
outside of Baghdád,

Bahá'u'lláh then did proclaim,

That He was the One, foretold by the Báb,

Exalted, to come in God's name.

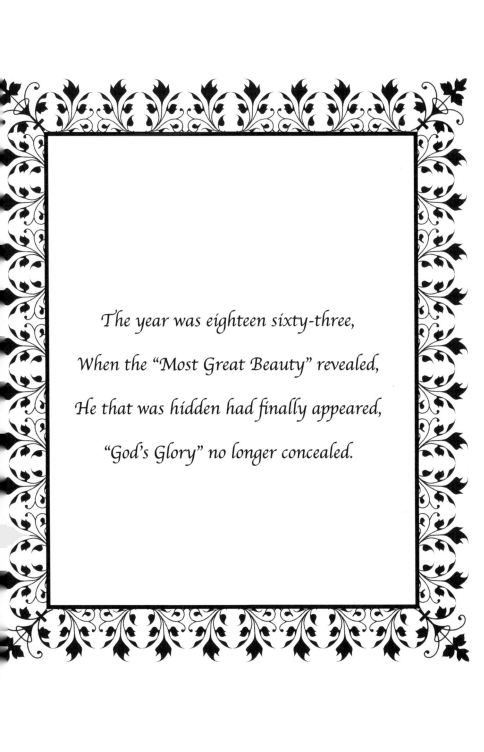

The year was eighteen sixty-three,

When the "Most Great Beauty" revealed,

He that was hidden had finally appeared,

"God's Glory" no longer concealed.

Twelve days in the garden,
soon ready to leave,

He mounted his trusty steed,

His friends had purchased
this stallion for Him,

The finest one of its breed.

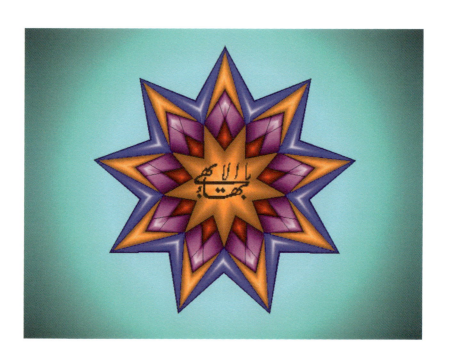

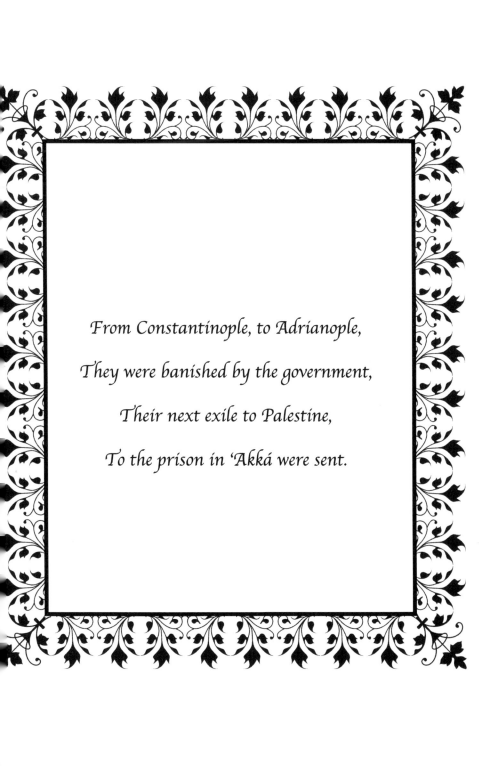

From Constantinople, to Adrianople,

They were banished by the government,

Their next exile to Palestine,

To the prison in 'Akká were sent.

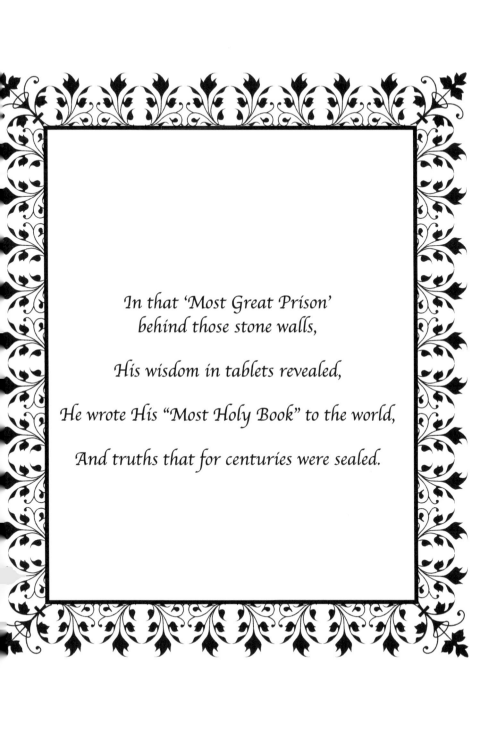

In that 'Most Great Prison'
behind those stone walls,

His wisdom in tablets revealed,

He wrote His "Most Holy Book" to the world,

And truths that for centuries were sealed.

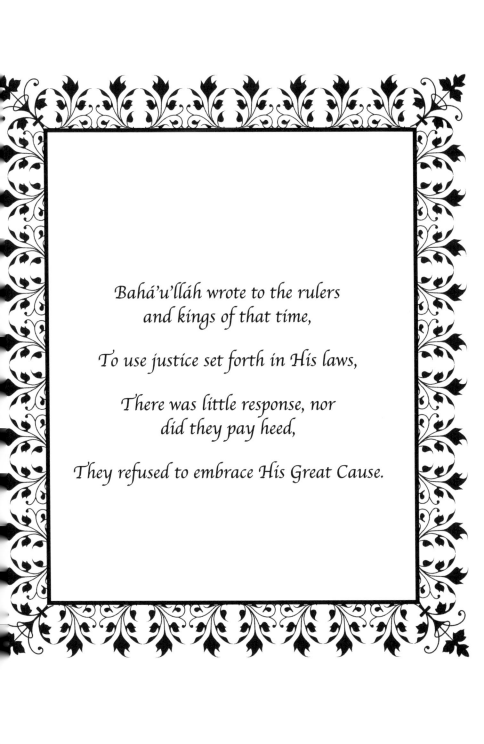

Bahá'u'lláh wrote to the rulers
and kings of that time,

To use justice set forth in His laws,

There was little response, nor
did they pay heed,

They refused to embrace His Great Cause.

After nine years in 'Akká,
He was finally set free,

An end to His sorrow and tears,

In the Mansion of Bahjí, near
the wide open plains,

He spent His remaining years.

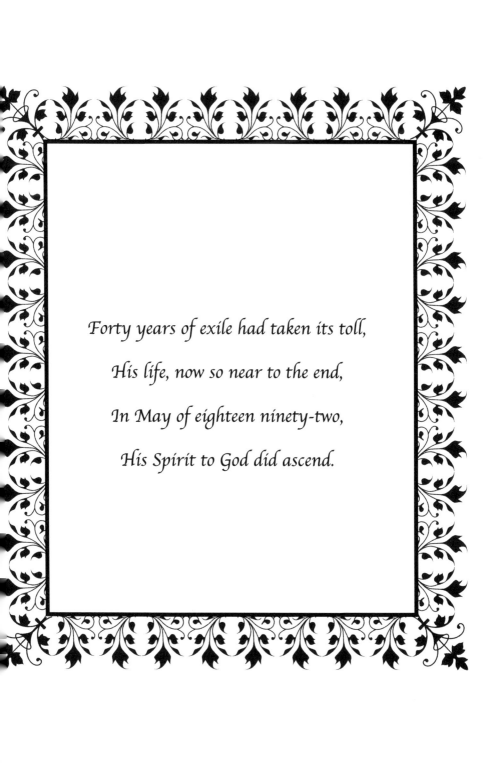

Forty years of exile had taken its toll,

His life, now so near to the end,

In May of eighteen ninety-two,

His Spirit to God did ascend.

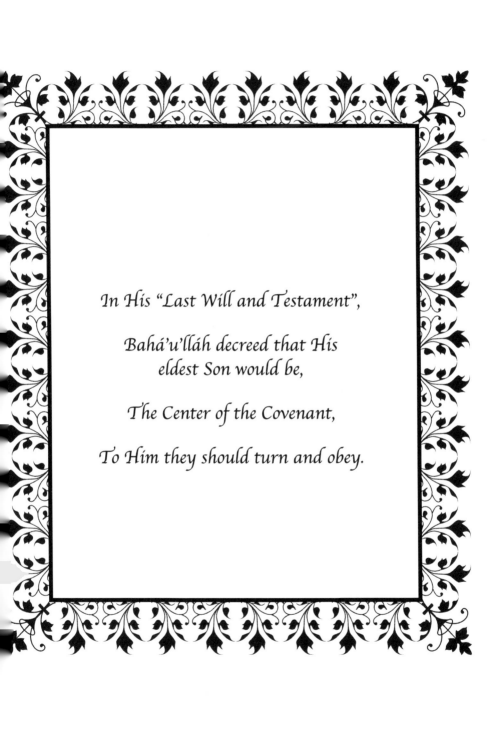

In His "Last Will and Testament",

Bahá'u'lláh decreed that His eldest Son would be,

The Center of the Covenant,

To Him they should turn and obey.

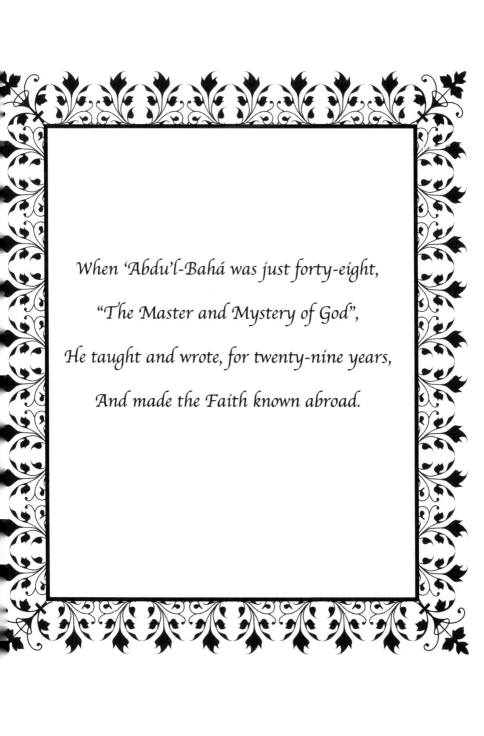

When 'Abdu'l-Bahá was just forty-eight,

"The Master and Mystery of God",

He taught and wrote, for twenty-nine years,

And made the Faith known abroad.

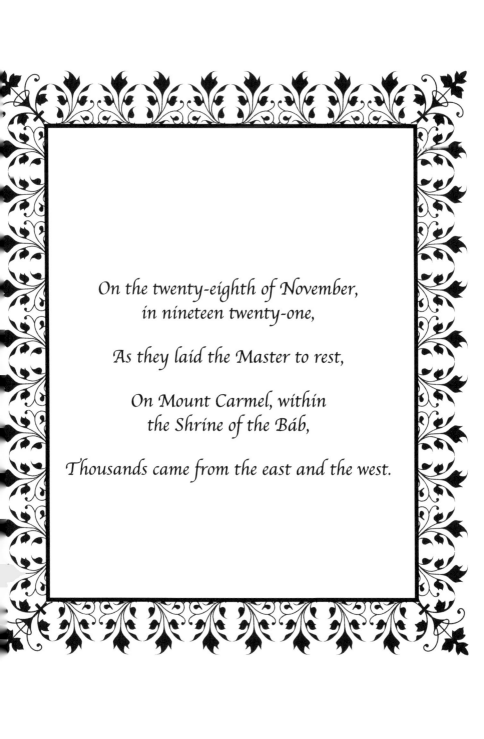

On the twenty-eighth of November,
in nineteen twenty-one,

As they laid the Master to rest,

On Mount Carmel, within
the Shrine of the Báb,

Thousands came from the east and the west.

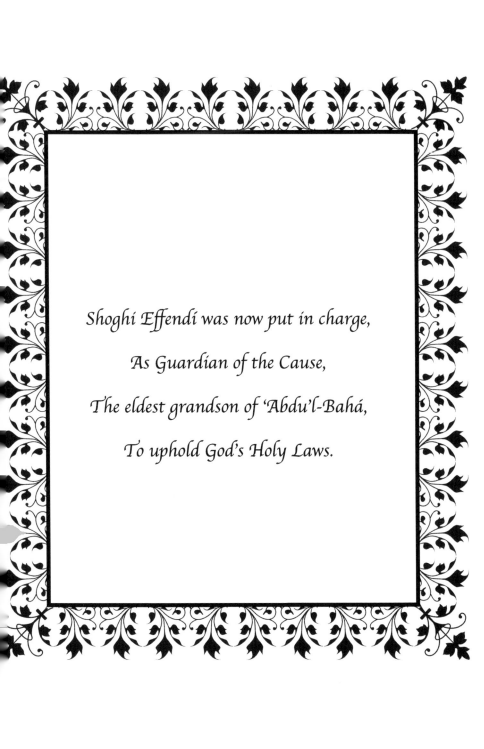

Shoghi Effendi was now put in charge,

As Guardian of the Cause,

The eldest grandson of 'Abdu'l-Bahá,

To uphold God's Holy Laws.

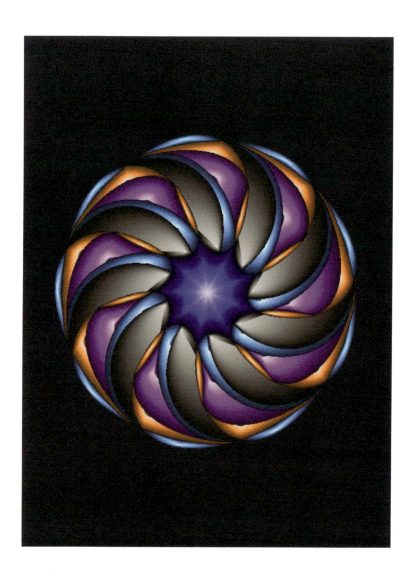

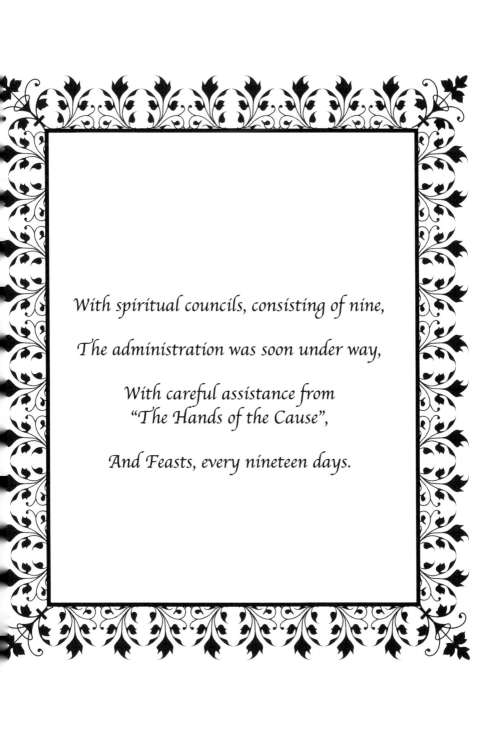

With spiritual councils, consisting of nine,

The administration was soon under way,

With careful assistance from
"The Hands of the Cause",

And Feasts, every nineteen days.

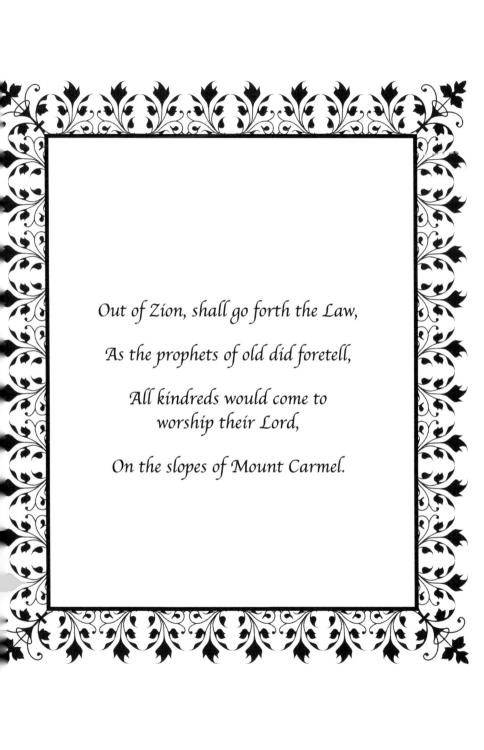

Out of Zion, shall go forth the Law,

As the prophets of old did foretell,

All kindreds would come to
worship their Lord,

On the slopes of Mount Carmel.

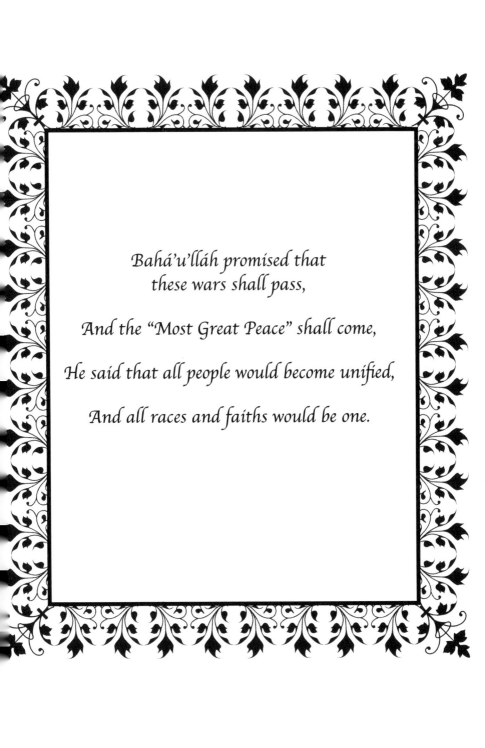

Bahá'u'lláh promised that
these wars shall pass,

And the "Most Great Peace" shall come,

He said that all people would become unified,

And all races and faiths would be one.

And yet there are people who
can't understand,

Why Bahá'ís are so happy and free,

They've heard the sweet
message of Bahá'u'lláh,

And that is like heaven to them and to me.

Compiled and written by Rubina Reierson

CPSIA information can be obtained
at www.ICGtesting.com
Printed in the USA
LVIW010357250712
291320LV00001B